Is the Bible Really a Message from God?

Ralph O. Muncaster

HARVEST HOUSE PUBLISHERS
Eugene, Oregon 97402

Cover by Terry Dugan Design, Minneapolis, Minnesota

By Ralph O. Muncaster

Are There Hidden Codes in the Bible?

Can You Trust the Bible?

Creation vs. Evolution

Creation vs. Evolution Video

How Do We Know Jesus Is God?

Is the Bible Really a Message from God?

What Is the Proof for the Resurrection?

IS THE BIBLE REALLY A MESSAGE FROM GOD?
Copyright © 2000 by Ralph O. Muncaster
Published by Harvest House Publishers
Eugene, Oregon 97402

Library of Congress Cataloging-in-Publication Data

Muncaster, Ralph O.
    Is the Bible Really a Message from God / Ralph O. Muncaster.
        p. cm.—(Examine the evidence series)
    ISBN 0-7369-0352-6
        1. Bible—Evidences, authority, etc. I. Title.
BS480 .M75 2000
220.1—dc21   99-053613

Printed in the United States of America.

00 01 02 03 04 05 06 07 08 09 / BP/ 10 9 8 7 6 5 4 3 2 1

Contents

Why Investigate the Bible?

If there is a God trying to communicate with us through the Bible, then it would be foolish not to be interested in the Bible.

For some it's a catch-22. They want evidence first, yet refuse to look to the Bible—which contains the evidence they need.

If the Bible is really the Word of God, the benefits of understanding it are immense.

- **It promises eternal life to anyone willing to take a few simple steps.**

- **It promises strength to face any challenges on a daily basis.**

- **It promises joy on earth and forever.**

Not bad promises, and fulfillment is not hard to obtain. God has concealed an incredible wealth of verification within the pages of the Bible—proof that: 1) He exists, 2) He wants to communicate with us, and 3) the Bible is the message system He uses. The proof is so overwhelming that only those absolutely committed to atheism can reject it—*providing they know of it.* For instance according to scientists, the probability that *prophecies fulfilled in the Bible* could have happened by chance is nil. Cross-referencing of evidence further confirms both the existence of God and the divine inspiration of the Bible.

Unfortunately, most people are unaware of the proof contained in the Bible. Popular media tends to present general opinion incorporating uninformed viewpoints. Realizing the incredible evidence of the Bible requires more depth than popular opinion. Only a small portion of evidence is summarized here. Hopefully, it will help encourage deeper investigation to know God through His Word. We are all without excuse for unbelief because evidence exists in abundance.

The Issues

The Bible has been analyzed *far* more than
any work in the history of the world.

1. Is the Bible Inspired by God?

Tremendous evidence exists that shows the Bible is inspired by
God. The design of the book, its miraculous survival, and
thousands of statistically improbable details verify God's
involvement (see pp. 8-11,22-31).

2. To What Degree? Ideas? Words? Details?

Probability analysis helps us find evidence of God throughout
the Bible. The exact words and letters indicate supernatural
design. Even people determining the selection of books for the
Bible must have been inspired by God. Numerous cross-references
of all books show amazing precision and divine design (see
pp. 30-45).

3. Is It Accurate?

Was the Bible originally recorded accurately? Evidence supports
the presence of God's hand in ensuring accuracy. There are many
instances of the Bible containing facts regarded as ridiculous at
the time, yet verified as fact today. Accuracy has been verified by
archaeology and science. And prophecy helps confirm divine
inspiration throughout the Bible (see pp. 22–45).

4. Was It Accurately Passed On?

The integrity of the early manuscripts has been confirmed by history along with modern archaeology and science. Large numbers of consistent ancient records were found in the Dead Sea Scrolls (similar in many respects to a time capsule). They are virtually identical to the Hebrew Bible of today (see pp. 10,11,28,29).

5. What Do I Do As a Result?

Discovering that the Bible is the inspired Word of God gives us the opportunity to have tremendous insight into the world around us. It clearly outlines the path to eternal life in heaven and teaches us how to maximize our opportunity to enjoy life on this earth (see pp. 46,47).

Miraculous Design

The Bible itself is a miracle—a miracle that is not obvious at first sight. But that miracle becomes apparent once facts are understood, and once the facts are considered in light of the *detailed, integrated information* that is cross-referenced throughout books written hundreds of years apart. Consider the following unlikely facts that describe the Bible's unique design.

1. *It consists of 66 books written by more than 40 authors from all walks of life.* The Bible is not an anthology carefully planned by some human publisher. Old Testament books were gradually added over many years by Jewish leaders. New Testament books were also written over many years and ultimately "canonized" by the church. Authors included:

   - Kings—David, Solomon
   - A political leader—Moses
   - A prime minister—Daniel
   - A Pharisee—Paul
   - A military general—Joshua

   - A shepherd—Amos
   - A tax collector—Matthew
   - A doctor—Luke
   - A cupbearer—Nehemiah
   - Fishermen—Peter, James, John

   An unlikely group to author the most revered book on earth!

2. *It was written over a span of 1500 years, in different places and situations.* It may seem easy for a group of different authors to meet at one time and in one event to construct an integrated, unified book. But how likely is it that vastly different authors would write hundreds of years apart under different situations and still be consistent? Some locations and situations included:

- In a palace—Daniel (540 B.C.)

- In a prison—Paul (A.D. 60)

- While traveling—Luke (A.D. 60)

- While fighting—Joshua (circa 1390 B.C.)

- In wilderness—Moses (circa 1430 B.C.)

- In a dungeon—Jeremiah (600 B.C.)

- In joy—David (1000 B.C.)

- In despair—David, Jeremiah

3. *It contains books of history, law, prophecy, poetry, proverbs, and songs.* Adding complexity to the divine design of the Bible are the vastly different styles in which various books are written. At first it might seem odd that such an unlikely combination of books would be grouped by anyone. Yet they miraculously tie together in theme, message, and even many detailed cross-references.

Why Would God Design Such Diversity?

To best communicate—A God who wants to communicate to all kinds of people in all kinds of situations would use all kinds of people in all kinds of situations. Writing styles are also designed to communicate different ways. What better communicates joy— a song or a legal report? What better emphasizes a point—a brief proverb or a detailed history?

To show divine planning—The incredible consistency of the Bible and the complex and detailed cross-referencing of information (a small portion of which is summarized in this book) could only occur with divine design.

Miraculous Survival

Certainly an all-powerful God could cause His
chosen Word (the Bible) to survive against all odds.
That's exactly what happened.

Weather could have destroyed it.

Unlike the clay tablets of the Babylonians, the holy Scriptures
had to be light and mobile. Papyrus and parchment were used
until paper was invented in A.D. 105. Many major ancient
writings written on such vulnerable material vanished altogether.
Yet there are a number of surviving manuscripts of the Old
Testament written before the birth of Christ. The Dead Sea Scrolls
alone consist of hundreds of manuscripts, including copies of
every book of the Old Testament (except Esther) (see pp. 28,29).

Weather *failed* to destroy God's Word.

Nations tried to destroy it.

Persecution of the Christians is well known. It started with the
Jewish leaders soon after the resurrection. Paul, a key Bible
author, was a leading murderer of Christians before experiencing
the risen Christ. Persecution from Rome became commonplace
after Nero's mass execution of Christians in A.D. 64. About 7
million graves in 900 miles of caves under the streets of Rome
(the Catacombs) attest to Rome's attempt to end Christianity.
Consequently, Christians were often cautious in expanding the
Word of God. Sometimes communication was cryptic. For
instance, some scholars believe the book of Revelation, written
by the apostle John in exile, was highly symbolic to help protect
its existence during a period of extreme persecution.

Nations *failed* to destroy God's Word.

Time might have destroyed it.

Many works of antiquity have simply disappeared over time. One scholar indicated that all works in existence from the A.D. 50s and 60s would fit between bookends placed a foot apart.[8] Even great works of history and literature have very few early manuscripts in existence. Unlike the Bible, the earliest extant copies of other great works were actually completed hundreds of years after the originals. The Bible has *many more copies* that were written *much closer* to the events they document.

Time *failed* to destroy God's Word.

MAJOR EXISTING MANUSCRIPTS[6]	EARLY RECORDS	YEARS FROM EVENT TO FIRST EXISTING MANUSCRIPT
Gallic Wars—Julius Caesar	10	1000
History—Pliny the Younger	7	750
History—Thucydides	8	1300
History—Herodotus	8	1300
Iliad—Homer (second most prevalent writing)	643	500
The New Testament	24,000+	25

In A.D. 303 an edict to destroy all Bibles was decreed by Rome. Anyone found with a Bible was killed.

How the Bible Fits with History

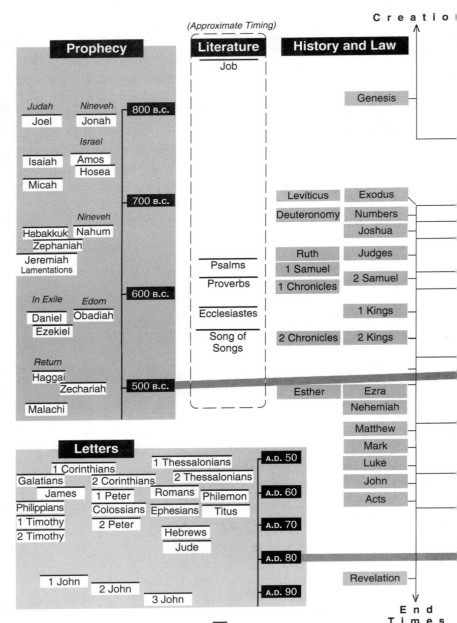

(Approximate Timing)

Prophecy | **Literature** | **History and Law**

Creatio

Job

Genesis

Judah — Joel   *Nineveh* — Jonah   **800 B.C.**

Israel
Isaiah — Amos / Hosea
Micah

700 B.C.

Leviticus   Exodus
Deuteronomy   Numbers
Joshua

Nineveh
Habakkuk — Nahum
Zephaniah
Jeremiah
Lamentations

Ruth   Judges
Psalms   1 Samuel   2 Samuel
Proverbs   1 Chronicles

600 B.C.

In Exile — Daniel   *Edom* — Obadiah
Ezekiel

Ecclesiastes   1 Kings
Song of Songs   2 Chronicles   2 Kings

Return
Haggai
Zechariah   **500 B.C.**

Esther   Ezra
Nehemiah

Malachi

Matthew
Mark

Letters

1 Corinthians   1 Thessalonians   **A.D. 50**
Galatians   2 Corinthians   2 Thessalonians   Luke
James   1 Peter   Romans   Philemon   **A.D. 60**   John
Philippians   Colossians   Ephesians   Titus   Acts
1 Timothy   2 Peter
2 Timothy   Hebrews   **A.D. 70**
Jude

A.D. 80

1 John
2 John   Revelation
3 John   **A.D. 90**

End
Times

12

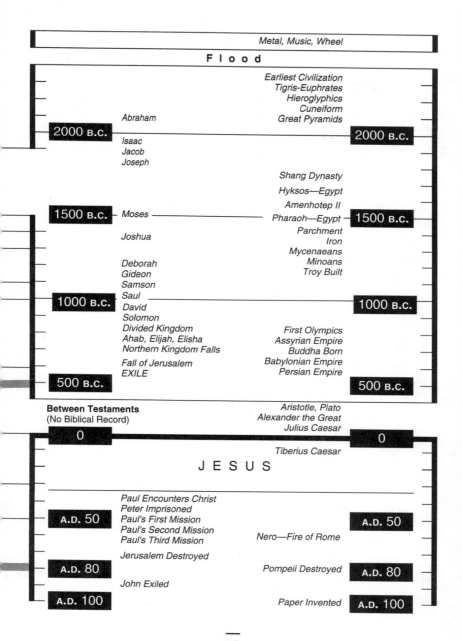

Metal, Music, Wheel

F l o o d

Earliest Civilization
Tigris-Euphrates
Hieroglyphics
Cuneiform
Great Pyramids

Abraham

2000 B.C.   2000 B.C.

Isaac
Jacob
Joseph

Shang Dynasty

Hyksos—Egypt

Amenhotep II

1500 B.C. — Moses ——————— Pharaoh—Egypt — 1500 B.C.

Parchment
Joshua   Iron
Mycenaeans
Deborah   Minoans
Gideon   Troy Built
Samson
Saul
1000 B.C. ———————————————— 1000 B.C.
David
Solomon
Divided Kingdom   First Olympics
Ahab, Elijah, Elisha   Assyrian Empire
Northern Kingdom Falls   Buddha Born
Fall of Jerusalem   Babylonian Empire
EXILE   Persian Empire
500 B.C.   500 B.C.

Between Testaments   Aristotle, Plato
(No Biblical Record)   Alexander the Great
                                  Julius Caesar
0   0

                                  Tiberius Caesar
J E S U S

Paul Encounters Christ
Peter Imprisoned
A.D. 50   Paul's First Mission   A.D. 50
Paul's Second Mission
Paul's Third Mission   Nero—Fire of Rome

Jerusalem Destroyed

A.D. 80   Pompeii Destroyed   A.D. 80

John Exiled

A.D. 100   Paper Invented   A.D. 100

Old Testament Overview
The Beginning

The Bible has thousands of verifiable facts that relate to world history. Archaeologists using the Bible have often found key information leading to important discoveries, including finding entire cities and cultures.

Genesis begins with a summary of how God created the heavens and earth. Thousands of years later, science has confirmed that the events of creation match the actual way the world was formed (see pp. 44,45). Genesis also reviews God's judgment of the world with the great flood—an event confirmed by accounts in virtually every society in the world. Geology and fossil records also offer strong flood evidence.

Not surprisingly, archaeology has defined the cradle of civilization as the Tigris-Euphrates valley. This lush valley was the richest, most habitable terrain just south of Mount Ararat—the resting place of Noah's ark. Archaeological evidence of early Genesis events in the region includes towers of Babel-type structures (Genesis 11) and very early metalworking and musical implements (Genesis 4:21,22). Genesis also describes the selection of Abraham to become father of a nation that would be *used to communicate God's message to the world.*

Among many things, God told Abraham to move hundreds of miles to a new promised land in Canaan. His hometown of Ur was in the Tigris-Euphrates area.

Genesis reviews how Abraham and Sarah gave birth to a miracle child, Isaac, the father of Jacob, who was the father of the 12 future leaders of the tribes of Israel. Egypt was a prominent power at the time, and the great pyramids were well under way.

Genesis ends with the account of how Joseph, sold as a slave by his brothers, became a powerful leader in Egypt and saved his family from famine. The entire family of Jacob moved to Egypt (where the Hebrew descendants eventually became slaves). Much of Genesis is a foreshadowing of the Messiah to come.

Archaeology confirms much historical information in Genesis, including the presence of Hebrews in Egypt, even in leadership positions. As important as the book's historical accuracy are the many prophecies hidden in Genesis that contain great details of the ultimate plan of God regarding the birth, life, and sacrifice of Jesus Christ.

Old Testament Overview
The Promised Land

The next four books—Exodus, Leviticus, Numbers and
Deuteronomy—complete the Torah (books of Law) written
by Moses about 1500 B.C. The books expand the important
concepts of:

1. God's deliverance of His nation by dramatic, miraculous
    events using ordinary people (Exodus).

2. God's law defined (Leviticus, Deuteronomy).

3. God's judgment exemplified (Exodus, Numbers).

4. God's prophecy of the Savior to come (all books).

Moses led the Israelites out of slavery in Egypt (highlighted by
God's miraculous parting of the Red Sea). The next 40 years of
wandering in the wilderness was an important time for God to
reveal His nature through the learning experiences of the nation.
The Bible makes this period of teaching available to all mankind.
Although the nation was being directed by God (a theocracy),
the Hebrew people had free will and often chose to disobey
God—suffering consequences as a result.

In the Land of Promise

Joshua led the Israelites into Canaan (now called Israel) as God
promised Abraham centuries before. At first, dramatic victories
followed the Hebrew people everywhere—victories that clearly
demonstrated God's power and fulfilled prophecy perfectly.
Archaeology has unearthed such things as the walls of Jericho
and other conquered cities, found precisely as indicated in the
Bible (see pp. 24,25).

The books of Judges and Ruth continue to elaborate on the early settlement in the land of Canaan. The time of Judges was one of increasing disobedience by Israel and was marred by problems both with neighboring enemies and within the tribes of Israel itself. The story of Ruth took place in the hills of Bethlehem. During a time when most of Israel was disobedient, Ruth (a Gentile) was obedient to God and was rewarded with a husband. Ruth became King David's great-grandmother and an ancestor of Jesus Christ.

The Kings

The historical books of Samuel, Chronicles, and Kings outline the period of the evolving Jewish nation during the time it was ruled by kings. Although God intended for himself to be the leader of the Jewish nation, the desire of the people to have a king was eventually granted by God. The kingdom of Israel was unified starting in 1050 B.C. under three successive kings: Saul, David and Solomon (each reigned 40 years). After Solomon the kingdom became divided in 930 B.C. Both Israel (the northern kingdom) and Judah (the southern kingdom) increasingly fell into apostasy. Israel was conquered by the Assyrians in 722 B.C., and Judah was exiled to Babylon starting in 606 B.C. (complete in 587 B.C.).

Old Testament Overview
God, Man, and Prophecy

The period of kings in Israel is an especially important time for the Bible's communication to man because:

- *It provided many real-life examples of interaction of man with God.* King David was considered a man after "God's own heart." He was frequently in God's favor and gave heartfelt praise and worship to God as recorded in many of the psalms. Yet David was also an adulterer and a murderer who suffered consequences for his actions like all humans. Despite this, David was revered by Israel and was a key ancestor of Jesus Christ. Many other examples, both good and bad, come from lives of people in this period.

- *It provided breadth of understanding of God.* Most psalms (songs), and other "poetry-style" books (Ecclesiastes, Proverbs, and Song of Songs) were produced during this period. This provides insight into different ways of understanding God. (Job, a unique book that gives particularly significant insight into suffering and evil, was probably written hundreds of years prior to this period.)

- *It provided books written specifically by "the prophets."* Seventeen books of prophecy were written during this period. Of the 300-plus prophecies contained in these books, many were immediately fulfilled (a prophet had to be 100-percent accurate or he was stoned to death). Others foretold incredible detail of the Savior who was to come (Jesus Christ).

Other Old Testament books—including Ezra, Esther, and Nehemiah—contain important facts of history that provide a complete picture of the historical scope and prophecy of the Bible. Ezra and Nehemiah deal with the return of Israel from exile, verifying precise fulfillment of prophecy. Esther shows God's care for Jews who did not return from exile.

Old Testament Summary

The Old Testament provides an in-depth view of the *nature of God*, the *nature of man* and a history of the *relationship of man and God*. It clarifies that man needs a Savior.

Equally important: It contains both a specific prophetic message of a Savior who was to come and a concealed prophetic message that would verify the information is in fact from God (providing future generations with assurance).

Between Testaments

The period between testaments was a time of great anticipation of the promised Messiah. During this period, the Rabbinic structure of the Jewish religion evolved. Also, strict rules and regulations were added, supplementing holy Scripture. This legalism caused much of Jesus' conflict with Jewish leaders.

New Testament Overview

The Gospels of Matthew, Mark, Luke, and John describe the life of Jesus on earth from four different perspectives. Matthew, a tax collector, wrote to show that Jesus was the promised Messiah and the "King." Mark described Jesus as the suffering servant, becoming the ultimate sacrifice for mankind. Luke, a physician, emphasized the human side of Jesus. And John focused on Jesus' deity. Even the difference in genealogical references reflect each viewpoint: Matthew—the legal line through Joseph ("husband of Mary," not the birth father); Mark—no genealogy (servant perspective); Luke—human ancestry through Mary; and John—a veiled reference to Jesus' divine heritage and preexistence.

All Gospels reveal the nature of Jesus through His teaching, His miracles, and the detailed account of His death and resurrection. All Gospels also reveal detailed fulfillment of Old Testament prophecy through Jesus. The book of Acts, written by Luke, reveals Jesus' impact after His resurrection. It confirms fulfillment of prophecies, including the appearance of Jesus in Galilee, the arrival of the Holy Spirit (Pentecost), the empowering of disciples to perform miracles in Jesus' name, and the church's rapid expansion.

The Letters

The remainder of the New Testament consists mostly of letters clarifying the role and teaching of Jesus. Paul, an avid enemy and murderer of Christians, converted immediately to Christianity upon encountering the risen Christ. He is responsible for at least 13 of the letters (books) of the New Testament. His two letters to the Thessalonians focus on the second coming of Jesus. His letters to the Corinthians, Galatians, Romans, Philippians, Colossians, and Ephesians all deal with problems of the new churches and believers. They explain doctrine as taught by Jesus and provide guidance for conduct of Christians and church leaders. Paul's individual letters to Timothy, Titus, and Philemon all had specific purposes. Letters to Timothy encouraged him and directed him in the path of becoming a good church leader. The letter to Titus instructed him in selection of church leaders and defined Christian behavior. The letter to Philemon requested assistance for a runaway slave (Onesimus) and exemplified the change Jesus Christ can make in a person.

Hebrews (writer unknown) defines the prominence of Jesus. His greatness is placed higher than that of Moses, Joshua, all prophets, all high priests, and even the angels. This placed Him in perspective for the Jews. James and Jude, written by natural half- brothers of Jesus (who became disciples *after* the resurrection) instruct believers on how to live their lives. Jude defines consequences for anyone guilty of false teaching and asks people to defend the true teaching of Jesus. Peter's and John's letters are instructional for believers.

The final book of the Bible, Revelation, was written by John in exile at the end of his life. It contains the detailed revelation that Jesus gave to John regarding the end of time. Revelation is written in a cryptic, symbolic style—perhaps due to the persecution at the time or perhaps because God had other reasons.

Can We Trust the Bible Record?

Billions of people have believed the
Bible is the inspired Word of God. The skeptic asks,
"Which Bible? There are many translations and versions."

The Bible God Inspired

If God inspired Scripture (which should become obvious), the
original written documents would be the inspired Word of God.
Later translations or "revisions" are the work of man. This is one
reason that some people still read the Old Testament in Hebrew
today. Other parts of the Bible were written in Aramaic and
Greek. Can we only benefit from the Bible if we speak Hebrew,
Greek and Aramaic? Of course not. The purpose of translation is
to make the message of the Bible available to everyone. However,
it's important to recognize that any translation could contain
man-made error. A reliable translation is based on thorough
analysis of the most accurate, and generally the *earliest available
manuscript—not a recent "revelation" that changes the meaning of the
original manuscript.*

Assuming that the original Scripture was the inspiration of God,
how do we know today's Bible is an accurate representation?
How do we know it was accurately copied? How do we know that
Scripture was not changed later to fit prophecy or ideas? There
are several reasons:[1]

- *Accountability of Scribes*—Being a Jewish scribe was among
  the most esteemed and demanding roles in biblical times.
  A lifelong commitment was required. Training started at
  age 14 and was not completed until age 40.

- *Scripture Copy Rules*—Master scrolls of Scripture had an
  incredible number of rules and cross-checks to assure accuracy in copying:

— Special surface preparation, inks

— Specified columns, 37 letters per line

— Only master used, no copies of copies

— Each letter visually confirmed

— Distance between letters checked

— Each letter of alphabet counted, verified

— Letters per page counted, verified

— Middle letter of scroll verified against master

— One mistake—*Entire scroll was destroyed* (if a master).

• *Internal Consistency*—There are thousands of cross-references within the Bible. After hundreds of years of review by millions of scholars, the Bible is still considered 100-percent internally consistent.

• *External Consistency*—Many skeptics and scholars have searched for inconsistencies of the Bible with the world. The Bible has always proved correct, sometimes before the world knew it.

• *Concealed "Hostile-Type" Prophecy*—The Bible contains many concealed prophecies contrary to the position of Judaism today. Any attempt to alter the record (Jews were the recordkeepers) would certainly have dealt with embarrassing doctrinal conflict—often requiring only a one-letter change.

• *Dead Sea Scrolls and Septuagint*—Dead Sea Scrolls buried for nearly 2000 years were found to match the current Scripture almost identically (see pp. 28,29). In a similar context, the original Hebrew Scripture was translated into Greek in 270 B.C. (the Septuagint). This early record provides another cross-check to current scriptural records.

Archaeology—Old Testament

Many people have attempted to discredit the Bible with archaeology. All have failed. One of the greatest archaeologists in history, Sir William Ramsay, devoted 30 years of his life trying to disprove Luke. Ramsay shocked the academic world when his work was finally published and he called Luke ". . . one of the greatest historians of all time." Ramsay then converted to Christianity.

Often scholars mistakenly assume the Bible is wrong only to be embarrassed by archaeology later. For example, the early Hittites were thought to be nonexistent in Abraham's time. Now entire museums of Hittite artifacts exist. Cities including Sodom and Gommorah were thought to be myths until evidence confirmed the existence of them. Today, virtually all reputable historians regard the Bible as an important, accurate historical document. Examples include: William F. Albright, Millar Burrows, F. F. Bruce, and Merrill Unger. As Unger states:

> ". . . Old Testament archaeology has rediscovered whole nations, resurrected important peoples, and in a most astonishing manner filled in historical gaps . . ."

Sample Archaeological Finds[3]

Jericho—The Bible records the amazing destruction of the walls of Jericho (Joshua 6). Excavation of Jericho identified the actual walls of Jericho that fell outward, allowing the Israelites to clamber over the ruins into the city as described in the Bible. In addition, large quantities of grain were found undisturbed—a highly unusual event for a city that was conquered. The Bible explains that God commanded the Israelites to leave things untouched other than valuable metals to be placed in the treasury (Joshua 6:17-19).

David[2]—In 1993 an inscription on a victory stele was found that referred to "the House of David" and to David as "king of Israel." This find corresponds to the defeat of Israel by the king of Damascus (1 Kings 15:20).

King Jehoiachin's Receipt— A fascinating receipt was discovered for a ration of oil, barley, and other food to King Jehoiachin, who was in captivity in Babylon. The receipt lists Jehoiachin, the king in Judah, and his five sons as recipients of the issues of food. The Bible indicates that the king of Babylon brought Jehoiachin out of prison and gave him a daily allowance for the rest of his life (2 Kings 25:27-30). On a separate stone tablet written in the seventh year of Nebuchadnezzar,[3] accounts of the fall of Jerusalem, the capture of Jehoiachin, and the appointment of a new king are recorded.

Joseph's Bones?[8]

A tomb in Shechem was revered for centuries as the burial place of Joseph. The Bible indicates Joseph's request to be returned to his home and how he was embalmed in Egypt (Genesis 50:25-26). Joshua further indicates that he was returned to Shechem (Joshua 24:32).

A few years before 1960 the tomb was opened. Inside was a body mummified according to Egyptian customs. The tomb contained other relevant items, including a sword of the type worn by Egyptian officials.

Thousands of similar archaeological finds exist
(see "Notes", p. 48, references 3, 4, 5).

Archaeology—New Testament

There are thousands of archaeological finds confirming or at least supporting most of the events of the New Testament. A few interesting examples include:

1. *Stable of Bethlehem*—Several sources indicate that a cave under the Church of the Nativity in Bethlehem was the birthplace of Jesus (caves were commonly used as stables). The site has never been seriously disputed by archaeologists.[4] Early authors (Jerome and Paulinus of Nola) indicate the site was marked at the time of Hadrian (A.D. 117–138). Such early identification is strong evidence.

2. *Synagogue in Capernaum*—The synagogue where Jesus taught and healed (Mark 1:21; 3:1-5; John 6:59) has probably been located. A site long revered as the authentic location was reexcavated in 1975, showing a foundation of a synagogue from the time of Jesus. First-century pottery confirmed the timing. It may have been the synagogue built by the centurion whose servant Jesus healed (Luke 7:1-5).

3. *Peter's House in Capernaum*—A probable site of Simon Peter's house has been found. Jesus visited Peter's house and may have used it as a home (Matthew 8:14; Mark 2:1). Its location (near the synagogue) and design are consistent with the Bible's description of Peter's house. In particular, the roof structure is of the same design as the one through which a paralytic was lowered to Jesus (see Mark 2:4). Excavations also revealed the site was considered an important religious site.

4. *Jacob's Well at Sychar*—The site of Jacob's well (John 4:1-42) has been identified. The well was functional in Jesus' day and matches the description in John 4:11. Wells were few and far between, and there is confirming evidence from writings and structures of early Christians pinpointing the site. Drinking water can still be drawn at the well.

5. *Pool of Siloam*—The site where Jesus healed a blind man (John 9:1-41) is well known. It was built by King Hezekiah around 800 B.C. (2 Kings 20:20).

6. *The Tomb of Lazarus*—(John 11:1-44) Bethany, the location of the tomb of Lazarus, is easily identified on the eastern slope of Mount Olivet about two miles from Jerusalem. An early author, Eusebius, writing in A.D. 330 identified the site of Lazarus' tomb. The same site is still widely regarded as authentic today. The burial chamber is only 8 feet square—entered through a 5-foot passageway.

Jesus' Burial Shroud?

A burial shroud (Shroud of Turin) is considered by many to be the actual burial shroud of Jesus (Matthew 27:59; Mark 15:46; Luke 23:53). Several items support its authenticity:

- Tests that confirm fiber type and small particles of limestone dust unique to the region.

- Confirmation of blood, in wounds precisely as indicated in the accounts of Jesus' unique execution.

- Confirmation of a crucifixion as a likely cause of the type of image created—matching a deceased body.

- Coins on eyes dated about the time of the crucifixion.

Some experts have been able to mimic creation of the shroud's image using today's technology. Some believe it to be a complex fourteenth-century hoax. The ultimate issue of its use by Jesus, however, will never be certain.

Dead Sea Scrolls and Key Manuscripts

Perhaps the most important archaeological find in history is the discovery of the Dead Sea Scrolls in 1947–48. Discovered accidently by a Bedouin shepherd searching a cave in the Qumran region near the Dead Sea, the scrolls were hidden by the Essenes (a Jewish sect similar to the Pharisees and Saduccees) just prior to the fall of Jerusalem in A.D. 70. It took almost 20 years to find all the scrolls and bring them together in one location.

What Are the Dead Sea Scrolls?

The discovery includes thousands of fragments and some complete scrolls found in 11 caves. About 800 scrolls have been identified, which include copies of every book of the Old Testament (except Esther) along with a number of other scrolls relevant to history and to the Essene community. The New Testament is not represented except for a few fragments believed to be from an early copy of Mark. Several scrolls have multiple copies. Many scrolls were written between 250 B.C. and 200 B.C.—long before fulfillment of the prophecies they contained about the coming Messiah (see p. 38).[4,6]

Luke—Original Writing

The original writing of Luke probably existed before A.D. 64. There is no mention of Nero nor mass executions in A.D. 64, which could hardly have been an oversight. Some believe Luke's writings were "legal-type" documents to help defend Paul.[9] Luke's accuracy is widely accepted.

The scrolls are written mostly in Hebrew, with some in Aramaic and a few fragments in Greek. Because of the vulnerability of papyrus, many of the scrolls deteriorated into fragments (except for some scrolls found in clay containers). There are, however, several completely intact scrolls in remarkably good condition. A complete scroll of Isaiah is now housed in the protective environment of the Shrine of the Book in Jerusalem.

Why the Scrolls Are Important

Discovery of the scrolls, which lay untouched for nearly 2000 years, provides absolute assurance that the Old Testament has remained virtually unchanged since long before the time of Christ. Not only were its books defined by that time, but comparison of Hebrew in the scrolls to present-day Hebrew copies of the Old Testament show almost letter-for-letter accuracy.

Septuagint

The Septuagint is the original translation of the Old Testament from Hebrew to Greek, from about 285 B.C. to 270 B.C. A few copies of this document written before Christ's birth still survive today. It provides yet another reference point that the detailed information of the Old Testament, including hundreds of specific prophecies about Jesus Christ, is authentic and was not merely added after the fact. As will be seen on pages that follow, much of the Old Testament contains subtle information relevant to Jesus Christ—something the Jews would have had no interest in confirming.

The Proof of Prophecy
Overview

People have always been fascinated with the future and with those who claim to foretell it. People look to the stars and to psychics and have many other ways of attempting to see what lies ahead. This is not new. God forbade such activity thousands of years ago and ordered that such people be put to death (Leviticus 19:31; 20:27). God did, however, command His people to listen to His prophets, who were defined to be 100-percent accurate.

How Important Is Prophecy?

God says prophecy confirms Him. It is the way man knows something is from God and God alone (Deuteronomy 18:17-22). Several times in the Bible it is the ultimate test of knowing something is from God (see Isaiah 41:22,23).

As a test of God's involvement, the Bible makes it clear that fulfillment of prophecy is more reliable than anything. It is more reliable than miracles, which might *seem* more spectacular. The Bible clarifies that miracles have been done by others (see Exodus 7:11) and even Satan performs "good" miracles (2 Corinthians 11:14). But only God can prophesy with 100-percent accuracy (see Isaiah 44:7,8). Hence, prophecy is *vitally important*. To emphasize it again:

**Only God can prophesy
with 100-percent accuracy.**

Peter, a man who was present during virtually all of the key miracles of Jesus, including the resurrection and the transfiguration, seemed to stress such ultimate importance of prophecy when he emphasized it *even above his own eyewitness testimony* (2 Peter 1:16-21).

The informed scientist and mathematician today would agree with God's standard for proof. Something that has *enormous* probability is really proof. As will be seen in the following pages, the Bible is filled with incredible prophecies and facts that meet both the statistician's and God's standards.

How Much Proof Is Really Proof?

If someone told you he could pick the winning lottery number, and then did, you might be impressed. Odds are maybe one in 10 million (which equals 1 in 10^7). Does that prove the person has divine knowledge? Maybe and maybe not, though it is very, very impressive. Now suppose he did it twice in a row. (One chance in 100 trillion, or 10^{14}.) It suddenly would seem obvious he had "special" information.

From a practical standpoint, scientists have determined that anything beyond one chance in 10^{50} is beyond reason— essentially impossible or absurd (like someone correctly picking the lottery 7 times in a row) . . . unless there is "special" knowledge involved.

Odds *far* more staggering than this describe prophecies and God's fingerprints in the Bible.

The Proof of Prophecy
People

Bible prophecies are of all types—information about *events* to occur, about *how* and *when* things will happen, and about specific *people*. Some prophecies were made about events that were imminent. Others were about events occurring hundreds of years later. "Prophets" who were wrong *once* in the short term were stoned, and their prophecies were not included in Scripture.

Bible Prophecies

The Bible contains more than 1000 prophecies: 668 are known to be fulfilled[10], with none ever proved false. (There are three that have not yet been confirmed.) Virtually all unfulfilled prophecies relate to the second coming of Christ and "end times."

Example

Cyrus (Isaiah 44:28)

Isaiah predicted that both Jerusalem and the temple would be destroyed—100 years before either happened. At the time, Jerusalem was strong and the temple was a major landmark. He further predicted a king named Cyrus would rebuild it—160 years before Cyrus was born.

Archaeology Confirms Cyrus' Decree

A stone cylinder was found that details many facts of Cyrus' reign including the decree to rebuild Jerusalem and the temple.[3]

Historically, Jerusalem and the temple were destroyed in 586 B.C. by King Nebuchadnezzar of Babylon. In 537 B.C., after Persia defeated Babylon, Cyrus the king decreed that Jerusalem and the temple be rebuilt.

Short-Term Examples

There are many other such prophecies in the Bible—some in the lifetime of eyewitnesses. Hence, they were confirmable by those recording them. False prophecy would certainly *not* be permitted in holy Scripture.

Deborah

- Promised victory over Sisera by a woman (Judges 4:9)— *fulfilled in Judges 4:21.*

Gideon

- Promised victory over Midian (Judges 6:14)—*fulfilled in Judges 7:1-25.*

David

- Bathsheba's child to die (2 Samuel 12:14)—*fulfilled in 2 Samuel 12:19.*

- Wives "violated" by son, seen by nation (2 Samuel 12:11, 12)—*fulfilled in 2 Samuel 16:22.*

Prophecy of Cyrus–God or Chance . . . ?

Estimated odds: One in 10^{14} —like correctly foretelling two lotteries in a row!

The Proof of Prophecy
Places

Examples

Tyre (Ezekiel 26:3-16)

In 586 B.C. (the eleventh year of the reign of Jehoiakim) the prophet Ezekiel was given a detailed prophecy regarding the powerful seaport of Tyre. At the time, Tyre was perhaps the strongest port in that part of the world. It could be compared to New York or Hong Kong of today. The prophecy in Ezekiel outlined several detailed fates that awaited Tyre:

Archaeology Confirms Ezekiel

Stone tablets have been found with a nearly complete text of Ezekiel dating from 600–500 B.C. (the time of Ezekiel). This verifies existence of the prophecy long before its fulfillment.

- Nebuchadnezzar would destroy the city on the mainland.
- More than one nation would come against it.
- The city would be flattened like the top of a bare rock.
- The area would become a site for spreading nets.
- Stones and timbers would be thrown into the water.
- The city would not be rebuilt.
- Nearby rulers would give up their thrones.

Historical Fulfillment—In 586 B.C., Nebuchadnezzar destroyed the mainland, forcing people to the island portion of the city. In 332 B.C., Alexander the Great began a siege of the island city. In order to reach it, he scraped the stones and timbers from the mainland city into the water to form a great causeway. Due to the successful siege, many neighboring rulers surrendered to Alexander without a fight. Today the ancient mainland portion of Tyre remains a flat rock where local fishermen dry out their nets.

Edom and Petra

Once a key trade waypoint and a city stronghold, the site would be:

- Unpopulated (Ezekiel 35:3,4, Jeremiah 49:18)—*fulfilled: Now barren, unpopulated.*

- Conquered by people of the east (Ezekiel 25:4)—*fulfilled: In sixth century B.C. by Nabateans.*

- Conquered by Israel (Ezekiel 25:14)—*fulfilled: Conquered by Hyrcanus, Simon of Gerasa.*

- Desolate to Teman (Ezekiel 25:13)—*fulfilled: Teman (on border) only populated city.*

- Inhabited by animals (Isaiah 34:11-15)—*fulfilled: Now home of lions, leopards, owls, goats.*

- Void of trade (Isaiah 34:10, Ezekiel 35:7)—*fulfilled: Now no people, no trade.*

Jeane Dixon—a Prophet?

Famous for the prediction that JFK would be elected and die in office (*Parade*, 1950) Jeane Dixon would hardly qualify as a biblical prophet.

First, odds were not amazing—1 chance in 5.

Second, many of her prophecies were wrong:

- World War III did not happen in 1954.

- Jackie Kennedy married Onassis the day after Dixon predicted she would never remarry.

- Vietnam war did not end in 1966 (it was 1975).

The Proof of Prophecy
Events

Examples

The Exile to Babylon and the Return (Jeremiah 25:9-11; Deuteronomy 28:49,50).

Both Moses and Jeremiah prophesied about the Hebrew nation being exiled to Babylon.[11] Not only do the prophecies contain very detailed information; they set the stage for the introduction of the Messiah.

It Was Predicted

- A foreign nation, speaking a different language, would defeat the Hebrew nation (Deuteronomy 28:49).

- They would destroy everything and not respect the elderly or pity the young (Deuteronomy 28:50,51).

- They would lay siege to cities (Deuteronomy 28:52).

- The Hebrews would resort to cannibalism (Deuteronomy 28:53).

- Judah would be exiled to Babylon (Jeremiah 25:9-11).

- After exile for *70 years* in "servitude," Babylon would be conquered and the Jews would return (Jeremiah 25:9-11).*

- After 70 years from the "desolation of Jerusalem" (Jeremiah 29:10-14), the final return from exile would be complete.*

* Note: Converting 360-day Jewish years to 365-day modern years yields exact fulfillment.

Historical Fulfillment

722 B.C.—Assyria defeats northern kingdom (Israel)

606 B.C.—"Servitude of the nation"—Nebuchadnezzar (Babylon) begins first siege of Jerusalem (Jeremiah 27:6-8; 29:10). Israel and King Jehoiakim of Judah exiled along with key leaders including Daniel (Daniel 1:1-4).

587 B.C.—"Desolations of Jerusalem"—Final siege of Jerusalem. Barbarianism of the Babylonians is detailed in several places including Lamentations (written in captivity): destruction (Lamentations 2:2-6), siege (Lamentations 3:5), slaughter of young and old "without pity" (Lamentations 2:21), and cannibalism (Lamentations 2:20).

537 B.C.—Jews return—decree of Cyrus 70 years after the first Jerusalem siege (Ezra 1—the beginning of the period of servitude).

517 B.C.—New temple complete. This completed the return exactly 70 years after the desolation of Jerusalem.

Second Exile

The second exile, in A.D. 70, and the return from all "directions" of the world were prophesied separately by Isaiah (Isaiah 11:11,12). Ezekiel also refers to the exiles returning from all nations (Ezekiel 37:21) and unifying Israel.

Establishment of the nation of Israel in 1948 and the return to Jerusalem in 1967 fulfill these prophecies. Like the first exile, it set the stage for another coming of Christ. The timing of each was predicted using prophecies in Ezekiel and Leviticus (summarized in reference 7).

The Proof of Prophecy
The Messiah

There are 322 prophecies regarding the Messiah in the Old Testament. The following decribes the Messiah *only from Old Testament prophecy.*

The Messiah will descend from Shem,[1] Abraham,[2] Isaac,[3] Jacob,[4] Judah,[5] Jesse,[6] and King David.[7] He will be born in the city of Bethlehem in the county of Ephrathah[8] when a bright star appears.[9] It will be a miraculous, virgin birth.[10]

The Messiah will be unique, having preexisted His birth.[8] He will perform many miracles: calming the sea[11] and causing the blind to see, the deaf to hear, the lame to walk, and the mute to talk.[12] He will be referred to in many ways including: God with us,[10] wonderful counselor, mighty God, everlasting Father and prince of peace.[13] One day He will rule over everything—all nations will bow down to Him.[14, 21]

The Messiah, however, will come to save mankind.[15] He will become man's sin offering[15] and present Himself to Jerusalem as both the anointed king[17] and the Passover lamb.[15] This will occur exactly 173,880 days after the decree by Artaxerxes to rebuild both Jerusalem and the Temple.[16] So, four days before passover, the Messiah will present Himself to a rejoicing Jerusalem riding on a

Location of Prophecy
(Partial Listing)

[1] Genesis 9,10
[2] Genesis 22:18
[3] Genesis 26:2-4
[4] Genesis 28:14
[5] Genesis 49:10
[6] Isaiah 11:1-5
[7] Samuel 7:11-16
[8] Micah 5:2
[9] Numbers 24:17
[10] Isaiah 7:14
[11] Psalm 107:29
[12] Isaiah 35:4-6
[13] Isaiah 9:6
[14] Isaiah 45:23
[15] Isaiah 53
[16] Daniel 9:20-27
[17] Zechariah 9:9
[18] Zechariah 11:12,13
[19] Isaiah 8:14
[20] Genesis 22
[21] Psalm 22
[22] Psalm 69:20-22
[23] Zechariah 12:10
[24] Psalm 41:9

donkey.[17] But then He will suffer greatly.[15] He will be rejected by many including His friends.[15] He will be betrayed by a friend[24] for 30 pieces of silver.[18] Later that money will be thrown on the floor of the temple[18] and will

God or Chance?

Estimated odds (48 prophecies): one in 10^{157}—like foretelling 22 lotteries in a row!

eventually go to a potter.[18] At His trial He will not defend Himself. He will say nothing[15] except as required by law. Israel will reject Him.[19]

The Messiah will be taken to a mountaintop identified by Abraham as "the Lord will provide."[20] There He will be crucified with His hands and feet pierced.[21] His enemies will encircle Him,[21] mocking Him, and will cast lots for His clothing.[21] He will call to God asking why He was "forsaken."[21] He will be given gall and wine.[22] He will die with thieves.[15] But unlike the thieves, none of His bones will be broken.[21] His heart will fail[21] . . . as indicated by blood and water spilling out[21] when He is pierced with a spear.[23] He will be buried in a rich man's grave.[15] In three days He will rise from the dead.[15,21]

Divine Design Evidence
Old Testament Tied to New Testament

Noah—Date of "Rebirth"

A seemingly insignificant detail showing divine design is found in Genesis 8:4. The Bible states:

> "The ark came to rest on the mountains of Ararat on the seventeenth day of the seventh month."

What does that signify? It signifies a new beginning for mankind. A "rebirth." And it ties in perfectly to the most important date in history (the day of the resurrection). In Noah's day, the seventh month was the Jewish month known as Nisan (it is still the seventh month on civil calendars). In Exodus, God told Moses to change Nisan to the first month for the religious year (Exodus 12:1,2). The New Testament reveals that Jesus was crucified on Passover (14th of Nisan) and rose from the dead three days later on the 17th of Nisan—the anniversary of Noah's "rebirth."

So the rebirth of mankind after Noah corresponds to exactly the same day of the year as the rebirth of mankind from the resurrection.[7]

Abraham—Foreshadowing the "Death and Resurrection"

At first the story of God's command to Abraham to sacrifice his son, Isaac, seems very puzzling (Genesis 22). After all, God abhorred the child sacrifices practiced by pagans of the day and commanded against them (Leviticus 18:21).

The book of Hosea indicates that God teaches through "parables told through the prophets" (Hosea 12:10). The sacrifice of Isaac is an example:

"Sacrifice" of Isaac

- Son born through miraculous birth (Genesis 18:11).

- Considered "only son" by God (Genesis 22:2).

- Son was to be sacrificed.

- Son carried wood up hill.

- Son "dead" in father's heart for three days (considered "dead" when the command was given).

- Son "resurrected" by substitution of ram.

- Isaac "disappears" from biblical account until "united" with his gentile bride Rebecca (Genesis 24).

Sacrifice of Christ

- Virgin birth (Matthew 1:18-20).

- Only son of God (John 3:16).

- Jesus was sacrificed.

- Jesus carried cross up hill.

- Jesus was "dead" for 3 days.

- Jesus resurrected. Was the substitute.

- Jesus ascends to heaven until united with His "bride" the church (Revelation 19:7).

Also consider . . .

- The *site* of the "sacrifice" of Isaac has been determined by some scholars to be Golgotha —the site of Jesus' crucifixion.[11]

- Abraham said God *"Himself"* would provide the offering (Genesis 22:8).

- The site was named *"the Lord will provide"* (Genesis 22:14).

Divine Design Evidence
Mathematical

The Number 7

For centuries, scholars have noticed the importance of the number 7 in the Bible. From the seven days of creation to the repeated use of "seven" in Revelation, the number signifies "completeness, perfection," and "of God."

Why Would God Use Number Patterns?

Perhaps God included evidence for scientifically oriented generations. Eyewitness testimony diminishes in acceptance (for some) after centuries. Scientific (statistical) evidence is now easier to analyze with computers.

Genesis, Matthew, the Bible

The first verse of the Old Testament (Hebrew) and first verses of the New Testament (Greek) indicate evidence of design that is *statistically beyond coincidence*. Both introduce God (at creation and with the genealogy of Jesus). And the number 7 is integrated throughout both—perhaps as a sign of completeness, perfection, and God.

The first verse of Genesis sets the stage for the heptadic structure of the Bible. Hebrew is read right to left, with no spaces or punctuation.

בראשיתבראאלהיםאתהשמיםואתהארץ

the earth (and) the heavens ("Elohim") God created (In) beginning

All of the Following Are Multiples of 7 in Genesis 1:1

Numeric Values*

- Number of words (7)

- Number of letters (28)

- Number of letters in subject, predicate (14)

- Number of letters in object phrase (14)

- Number of letters in "the heavens" (7)

- Number of letters in "the earth" (7)

- First, middle, and last letters (7x19)

- First and last letter of all words (7x199)

- First and last letter of first, last word (7x71)

- First and last letter of all other words (7x129)

- The verb "created" (7x29)

The Genealogy of Jesus[11]—Multiples of 7 (Matthew 1:1-17)

- Number of words

- Number of letters

- Number of vowels

- Number of consonants

- Number of words starting with a vowel

- Number of words starting with a consonant

- Number of names

- Number of male names

- Number of letters in the three female names

- Number of compound words

- Number of nouns

- Number of words that are not nouns

- Number of times the most frequent word is used.

- Number of words occurring only once

- Number of words occurring more than once

- Number of letters in name of only city listed

Odds of coincidence are nil.

*Note: All Hebrew letters have a numeric value. Numerals were not used.

Science and the Bible

The Bible is not a book about science. Nevertheless,
we should expect it to be accurate—even though it
was written thousands of years ago. In fact, it is.

Creation Events (Genesis 1)

Reviewing the *order of events* of creation shows the Bible is
accurate as far as science can verify. It's important to notice the
vantage point of "God's spirit"—hovering over the waters (Genesis
1:2):

Events of Creation (confirmed by science)[12]

1. *Heavenly bodies created* (Genesis 1:1)—The earth was initially
    covered with a thick layer of gas not allowing light to pen-
    etrate.

2. *"Let there be light"* (Genesis 1:3)—The atmosphere was altered
    to allow some light to reach the surface of the water (critical
    for photosynthesis).

3. *Development of hydrologic cycle* (Genesis 1:6)—The water cycle
    was a critical prerequisite for life of any type.

4. *Formation of land and sea* (Genesis 1:9,10)—An event neces-
    sary for development of land life.

5. *Creation of vegetation* (Genesis 1:11)—Scientists agree this was
    the first life form.

6. *Atmosphere transparency* (Genesis 1:14)—Changes allowed
    light to directly penetrate the atmosphere. "Lights in the
    heavens" became visible, marking day and night and seasons.

7. *Creation of small sea animals and birds* (Genesis 1:20)—Scientists agree the first animal life was in the sea, with birds following.

8. *Creation of land animals* (Genesis 1:24)—The final life forms prior to man. Genetics ("according to its kind") were accurate.

9. *Creation of man* (Genesis 1:26)—Final creature appearing on earth.

Earth Described as Spherical

People thought the earth was flat. The Bible indicates a sphere (Isaiah 40:22). (Note: Some Bibles translate the Hebrew word "khug" as "circle." "Sphere" is more precise.)

Stars Determined Uncountable

At a time when people believed there were 1100 stars, the Bible said stars were "uncountable" (Jeremiah 33:22). We know there are at least 100 billion stars in 100 billion galaxies. Counting them at a rate of 10 per second would take more than 100 trillion years, making it impossible to "count" them.

Einstein Discovers Bible Truth

Newton's physics fell far short of biblical statements. Einstein's discovery of general relativity is consistent with Bible claims. Einstein died begrudgingly admitting the probability of a creator.[12]

Common Questions

What If I Don't Believe the Entire Bible?

Having a relationship with God does not depend on believing the entire Bible. Belief in Jesus as Savior and asking Him to be director of your life are all that is required. Some people wonder why God uses prophecy and sometimes cryptic wording. There is no absolute answer to this. Perhaps God wants people to seek Him and then find Him. Perhaps He wants to emphasize faith. Or perhaps He wants to allow the Holy Spirit to reach people differently. Even so, general evidence is also abundant.

How Can We Ensure the Right Relationship to Go to Heaven?

When Jesus said not all who use His name will enter heaven (Matthew 7:21-23), He was referring to people who think using Christ's name along with rituals and rules is the key to heaven. A *relationship* with God is not based on rituals and rules. It's based on grace and forgiveness, and the right kind of relationship with Him.

How to Have a Personal Relationship With God

1. Believe that God exists and that He came to earth in the human form of Jesus Christ (John 3:16; Romans 10:9).

2. Accept God's free forgiveness of sins through the death and resurrection of Jesus Christ (Ephesians 2:8-10; 1:7,8).

3. Switch to God's plan for life (1 Peter 1:21-23; Ephesians 2:1-5).

4. Express desire for Christ to be director of your life (Matthew 7:21-27; 1 John 4:15).

Prayer for Eternal Life with God

"Dear God, I believe You sent Your Son, Jesus, to die for my sins so I can be forgiven. I'm sorry for my sins and I want to live the rest of my life the way You want me to. Please put Your Spirit in my life to direct me. Amen."

Then What?

People who have sincerely taken the above steps automatically become members of God's family of believers. A new world of freedom and strength is available through prayer and obedience to God's will. New believers also can build their relationship with God by taking the following steps:

- Find a Bible-based church that you like and attend regularly.

- Try to set aside some time each day to pray and read the Bible.

- Locate other Christians to spend time with on a regular basis.

God's Promises to Believers

For Today
But seek first His kingdom and His righteousness, and all these things [things to satisfy all your needs] will be given to you as well.
—Matthew 6:33

For Eternity
Whoever believes in the Son has eternal life, but whoever rejects the Son will not see life, for God's wrath remains on him.
—John 3:26

Once we develop an eternal perspective, even the greatest problems on earth fade in significance.

Notes

1. McDowell, Josh, and Wilson, Bill, *He Walked Among Us*, Nashville, TN: Thomas Nelson, Inc., 1993.

2. Orange County *Register*, August 6, 1993.

3. Free, Joseph P., and Vos, Howard F., *Archaeology and Bible History*, Grand Rapids, MI: Zondervan, 1969.

4. McRay, John, *Archaeology and the New Testament*, Grand Rapids, MI: Baker Book House, 1991.

5. Youngblood, Ronald F., *New Illustrated Bible Dictionary*, Nashville, TN: Thomas Nelson, Inc., 1995.

6. Shanks, Hershel (ed.), *Understanding the Dead Sea Scrolls*, New York, NY: Vintage Books, 1993.

7. Missler, Chuck, *Footprints of the Messiah*, Audio Tape, Coeur d'Alene, ID: Koinonia House, Inc. 1994.

8. McDowell, Josh, and Wilson, Bill, *A Ready Defense*, San Bernardino, CA: Here's Life Publishers, Inc., 1990.

9. Missler, Chuck, *A Walk Thru the Bible*, Audio Tape, Coeur d'Alene, ID: Koinonia House, Inc., 1994.

10. Walvoord, John F., *The Prophecy Knowledge Handbook*, Wheaton, IL: Victor Books, 1984.

11. Eastman, Mark, M.D., and Missler, Chuck, *The Creator Beyond Time and Space*, Costa Mesa, CA: The Word for Today, 1996.

12. Ross, Hugh, Ph.D., *The Fingerprint of God*, Orange, CA: Promise Publishing Co., 1989.

Bibliography

Blandenbaker, Francis, *What the Bible Is All About*, Quick Reference Edition, Ventura, CA: Regal Books, a division of Gospel Light, 1989.

Encyclopedia Britannica, Chicago, IL: 1993.

Josephus, Flavius. Translated by Whiston, Wm., *The Complete Works of Josephus*, Grand Rapids, MI: Kregel, 1981.

Muncaster, Ralph O., *Jesus—Investigation of the Evidence*, Newport Beach, CA: Strong Basis to Believe, 1996.

Reader's Digest, *ABCs of the Bible*, Pleasantville, NY, 1991.

Reader's Digest, *Who's Who in the Bible*, Pleasantville, NY, 1994.

Rosen, Moishe, *Y'shua*, Chicago, IL: Moody Bible Institute, 1982.

Smith, F. LaGard, *The Daily Bible in Chronological Order*, Eugene, OR: Harvest House, 1984.